Surprise and Flexibility

CAUSES & EFFECTS OF EMOTIONS

CAUSES & EFFECTS OF EMOTIONS

Surprise and Flexibility

Rosa Waters

Mason Crest

Mason Crest
450 Parkway Drive, Suite D
Broomall, PA 19008
www.masoncrest.com

Printed and bound in the United States of America.

First printing
9 8 7 6 5 4 3 2 1

Series ISBN: 978-1-4222-3067-1
ISBN: 978-1-4222-3080-0
ebook ISBN: 978-1-4222-8773-6

The Library of Congress has cataloged the
hardcopy format(s) as follows:
        Library of Congress Cataloging-in-Publication Data

Waters, Rosa, 1957-
  Surprise and flexibility / Rosa Waters.
     pages cm. — (Causes & effects of emotions)
  Audience: Grade 7 to 8.
  Includes index.
  ISBN 978-1-4222-3080-0 (hardback) — ISBN 978-1-4222-3067-1 (series)
1. Surprise—Juvenile literature. 2. Emotions—Juvenile literature. 3. Adaptability (Psychology)—Juvenile literature. I. Title.
  BF575.S8.W38 2014
  152.4—dc23
                   2014005511

CONTENTS

KEY ICONS TO LOOK FOR:

Text-Dependent Questions: These questions send the reader back to the text for more careful attention to the evidence presented there.

Words to Understand: These words with their easy-to-understand definitions will increase the reader's understanding of the text, while building vocabulary skills.

Series Glossary of Key Terms: This back-of-the book glossary contains terminology used throughout this series. Words found here increase the reader's ability to read and comprehend higher-level books and articles in this field.

Research Projects: Readers are pointed toward areas of further inquiry connected to each chapter. Suggestions are provided for projects that encourage deeper research and analysis.

Sidebars: This boxed material within the main text allows readers to build knowledge, gain insights, explore possibilities, and broaden their perspectives by weaving together additional information to provide realistic and holistic perspectives.

INTRODUCTION

The journey of self-discovery for young adults can be a passage that includes times of introspection as well joyful experiences. It can also be a complicated route filled with confusing road signs and hazards along the way. The choices teens make will have lifelong impacts. From early romantic relationships to complex feelings of anxiousness, loneliness, and compassion, this series of books is designed specifically for young adults, tackling many of the challenges facing them as they navigate the social and emotional world around and within them. Each chapter explores the social emotional pitfalls and triumphs of young adults, using stories in which readers will see themselves reflected.

Adolescents encounter compound issues today in home, school, and community. Many young adults may feel ill equipped to identify and manage the broad range of emotions they experience as their minds and bodies change and grow. They face many adult problems without the knowledge and tools needed to find satisfactory solutions. Where do they fit in? Why are they afraid? Do others feel as lonely and lost as they do? How do they handle the emotions that can engulf them when a friend betrays them or they fail to make the grade? These are all important questions that young adults may face. Young adults need guidance to pilot their way through changing feelings that are influenced by peers, family relationships, and an ever-changing world. They need to know that they share common strengths and pressures with their peers. Realizing they are not alone with their questions can help them develop important attributes of resilience and hope.

The books in this series skillfully capture young people's everyday, real-life emotional journeys and provides practical and meaningful information that can offer hope to all who read them.

It covers topics that teens may be hesitant to discuss with others, giving them a context for their own feelings and relationships. It is an essential tool to help young adults understand themselves and their place in the world around them—and a valuable asset for teachers and counselors working to help young people become healthy, confident, and compassionate members of our society.

Cindy Croft, M.A.Ed
Director of the Center for Inclusive Child Care at Concordia University

Words to Understand

researchers: Scientists who try to make new discoveries.

evolution: The process by which organisms slowly change to adapt to their environments over long periods of time.

categories: Classes or divisions that things are seperated or sorted into.

neurologists: Scientists or doctors who study the brain and nervous sytem.

automatic: Happening on its own, without being controlled by someone or something else.

stimulus: Something that causes a reaction.

psychologists: Experts on the human mind and emotions.

predictable: Having a result that you would expect.

ONE

WHAT IS SURPRISE?

"Suppise!" Two-and-a-half-year-old Jeremy leaps up from behind the sofa and startles his mother. When she jumps in surprise, letting out a little squeak, Jeremy rolls on the floor giggling.

Jeremy has already learned that "surprise" is the emotion people feel when something unexpected happens. Over the past year or so, Jeremy has also learned the names for many other emotions. He probably started out with the most basic ones—"sad" and "happy." Then he may have learned "angry" and "scared." As he learns more and more words, he will be able to put names to more and more of the feelings he experiences inside.

WHAT ARE EMOTIONS?

Researchers have discovered that all our emotions—including surprise—are produced within our brains. Scientists have been

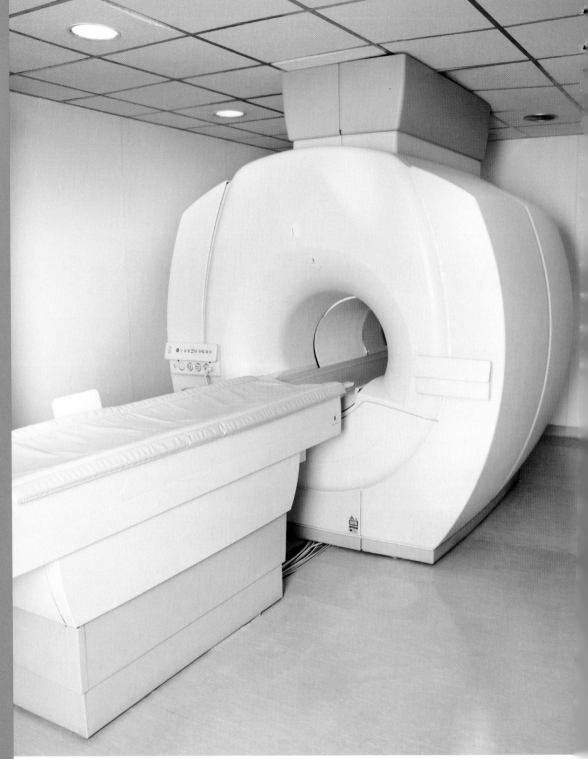

An MRI machine looks like this. The person will lie with the part of her body that's being examined inside the donut. It doesn't hurt—and it lets doctors and researchers actually look inside a person's brain.

Make Connections

Magnetic resonance imaging (MRI) is a test that uses a magnetic field and pulses of radio wave energy to make pictures of organs and structures inside the body. For an MRI test, the area of the body being studied is placed inside a special machine that contains a strong magnet. Pictures from an MRI scan are digital images that can be saved and stored on a computer for more study.

working to map the human brain, identifying which parts of our brains do what. They have found that human emotion is a pleasant or unpleasant sensation that's created in the brain's limbic system. When scientists look at an MRI of a person's brain when she's feeling emotions, they can actually see the different parts of her brain lighting up as they become more active.

All this has been going on inside our brains throughout our entire lives, ever since we were babies. Sometimes we feel happy, and sometimes we feel sad; sometime we feel angry, sometimes we're scared, and sometimes we are bored. All these feelings come and go inside us. When we were very young, though, we didn't have words for all these feelings. As we grew older, like Jeremy, we learned to put words to our feelings.

At their most basic level, however, these feelings have no words. They're simply sensations. Human beings have given these various brain sensations labels (such as amusement and anger, disgust and embarrassment, fear and guilt, happiness and hate, love and sadness, shame and surprise). Meanwhile, as we experience these feelings, chemicals inside our brains are making our brain cells behave in specific ways.

These brain responses do an important job. They direct our attention toward things that are important. When something makes

LIMBIC SYSTEM STRUCTURES

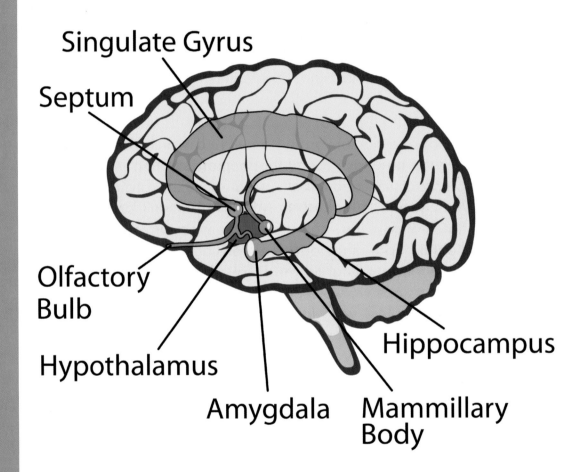

All these structures within the brain are part of the limbic system.

Make Connections

The limbic system is a set of brain structures located on top of the brainstem and buried under the brain's gray matter. Limbic system structures are involved in many of our emotions, including fear, anger, and pleasure. Other structures within the limbic system have to do with memory and our sense of smell.

us happy, for example, our brains says, "Notice this! Try to get more of this in your life!" Or when something scares us, the reaction in our brains tells us, "Be careful!"

Scientists believe that we have *evolution* to thank for the emotions we feel today. Long, long ago, the human beings who had these reactions inside their brains were able to avoid danger better. As a result, they lived longer than their companions who lacked these reactions. Because they lived longer, they were able to have children—and they passed along this trait to their children, who in turn passed it along to their children.

Emotions helped early humans respond to the world around them. They were survival mechanisms that helped the human race survive. Today, emotions continue to play important roles in human life.

WHAT MAKES SURPRISE DIFFERENT FROM OTHER EMOTIONS?

We often put emotions into *categories*—positive (good) emotions and negative (bad) emotions. We think of happiness, amusement, and love as positive emotions, and we usually consider sadness, fear, and hate to be negative feelings. All of these emotions, both

Not all surprises are good ones!

Make Connections

We often think of "chemicals" as a special kind of substance—but really, everything in the world is made up of chemicals! Everything you touch and taste is a chemical. Water is a chemical. Paper is made up of chemicals. So are you!

When scientists study chemicals, they're studying the way things interact with each other. Inside your body, for example, certain chemicals combine with other chemicals—and when that happens, they change each other.

positive and negative, do important jobs in our lives, but some emotions feel pleasant to us, while others may feel painful or uncomfortable. Surprise is the only emotion that is neutral, neither good nor bad. It's usually mixed with other emotions.

Imagine you open a card from your grandmother and discover that out of the blue, for no particular reason, she's sent you a check for $50. You're surprised—and happy, because now you can afford to buy something you've been saving for.

Now think about another scenario. You're walking down the street, when suddenly a very large, growling dog leaps in front of you with its teeth bared. You're surprised—and terrified.

Or say things seem to be really good between you and your girlfriend. You feel as though the two of you are getting closer and closer. Then one afternoon when the two of you are hanging out together, she turns to you and tells you she wants to start seeing other people. You're surprised—and heartbroken.

Researchers tell us that surprise is the fastest of all the emotions. It only lasts for a few seconds—and then it usually turns into something else, like sadness or fear, happiness or anger. Surprise

Playing peekaboo is one of a baby's first experiences with surprise. It's a game that almost all babies love—being surprised and surprising others makes them laugh.

Make Connections

We use language to express different "shades" of emotion. All these words describe some kind of surprise.

amazed	astonished	startled
flabbergasted	stunned	astounded
dumbfounded	stupefied	staggered

can make us laugh, as when a clown does something unexpected. It might make us angry, like when someone gives us an unexpected shove when we're standing in a line.

SURPRISE AND THE BODY

Neurologists believe that surprise is related to the body's startle response. This is what happens to you when someone jumps at you and shouts, "Boo!" It's what little Jeremy's mother experienced when her son popped up from behind the sofa. It's an **automatic** response of the brain and the body to any sudden and unexpected **stimulus**, such as a flash of light, a loud noise, or a quick movement.

When we're startled, the muscles in our arms and legs contract (getting us ready to run away, if necessary). We blink (to protect our eyes, in case something comes flying at us). Our blood pressure goes up, sending more blood to our muscles (again, just in case we need to run away). We breathe faster and our heart rate increases, sending out more oxygen to our bodies. All that happens very fast. In fact, scientists have found that it takes less than two-tenths of a second for the entire startle response to occur! Afterward, usually, everything goes back to normal. Our muscles relax. Our heart rate, blood pressure, and breathing return to their usual levels.

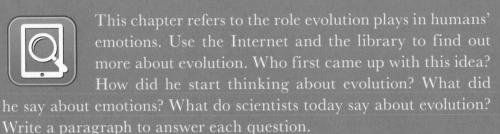

The startle response serves an important function. It gets our attention. It interrupts whatever we've been thinking about and forces us to focus on something new. Once we've shifted our attention, a new emotion will often take over, depending on the situation.

SURPRISE AND PSYCHOLOGY

Psychologists look at surprise a little differently from neurologists. Neurologists focus on what's going on inside the body's nervous system, while psychologists think about how human emotions interact and affect life. From a psychological perspective, surprise is what happens when life turns out differently from what we had expected.

Humans tend to make up rules about how life works:

The sun rises in the morning.
Dogs bark, and cats meow.
Rainy days are sad.
Some people are nice, others are mean.

These rules may or may not be correct—or they may be correct much of the time, but not all the time. All of us may have a slightly

Text-Dependent Questions

1. How does this chapter define the word "emotion"?

2. Explain what an MRI does.

3. Describe how evolution and emotions are connected.

4. List the things that happen within your body when you're startled.

5. Define "surprise" from a psychologist's perspective.

different set of rules we've built up in our minds over the course of our lives. These rules help us know what to expect in life. They help us feel more in control.

When something happens that goes against these rules, we're surprised. We had assumed that the world worked one way—and then it turned out to not be that way after all. The person we thought was mean did something really kind. Something good happened on a rainy day. Imagine our surprise if our dog meowed!

Some people like to be surprised. They find it funny or exciting or simply interesting. They may seek out experiences where they're likely to encounter the unexpected. Other people, however, are uncomfortable with surprise. It may make them feel anxious or stressed. They like life to be **predictable**. Psychologists say that people who are comfortable with surprise are more emotionally flexible than people who aren't.

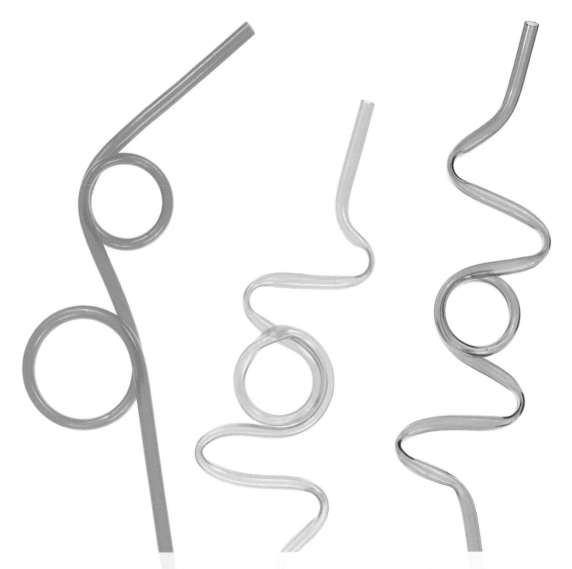

Words to Understand

adapt: Change to account for something new.
inconvenient: Causing trouble or discomfort.
reliable: Consistently good or high quality.
options: Choices.
repertoire: The selection of things someone is good at or is able to do without notice.

TWO

WHAT IS FLEXIBILITY?

Sarah and her friend Shannon have very different approaches to life. Shannon likes to have a plan in place every day. She wants to know exactly what she's doing every minute of the day. Of course things often come up that keep her plans from going smoothly—and when that happens, Shannon gets very upset. Meanwhile, Sarah likes to take life easy. She allows room in her day for the unexpected—and when things do take her by surprise, she's able to take it in stride, without being thrown off balance.

Today is no exception. As the two girls walk into school together, Sarah's feeling a little on edge, but she knows it's because she didn't have time to eat breakfast. She'll just have to get through the next couple of hours until her lunch period, and then, once she's eaten, she knows she'll start feeling better. In the meantime,

SURPRISE AND FLEXIBILITY

Sometimes life can feel so overwhelming you want to scream, but reacting with anger isn't the best way to deal with the stress.

How we react to the things that happen to us is often up to us. There's no use crying over spilled milk!

though, Shannon is really getting on her nerves. Sarah reminds herself not to say much until after she's had a chance to eat something. That way, she won't say anything mean to her friend.

So as they walk to their lockers, Sarah just says, "Mm-hm," while her friend complains about the fight she had with her mother. "Mmm," she says when Shannon tells her that her mother is going to ruin her entire life. And when Shannon drops her purse on the floor and screams in frustration, Sarah just gets down on her knees and helps her friend pick up her things. But as Sarah turns the combination on her locker, she really wishes Shannon's voice wasn't quite so loud sometimes.

The boxer who can roll with the punches stays on his feet no matter what's thrown at him.

Just as Sarah thinks that, Shannon lets out an even louder shriek and kicks her locker. "It's jammed! I can't believe it! The stupid thing is jammed!"

While Shannon bursts into tears, Sarah looks at her friend for a moment. Then she says quietly, "Tell me your combination."

"There's no point!" Shannon insists through her tears. "It's jammed. Now I'm going to be late for math class. Mrs. Bucci will yell at me for being late. What a horrible, horrible day. I *hate* my life!" She leans against the lockers and sobs.

Sarah sighs. "It's not the end of the world, Shannon. Just tell me your combination."

Finally, Shannon manages to say the numbers between her sobs. Sarah turns the combination lock slowly and carefully—and then opens the door. "There you go, Shannon." She gives her friend a hug. "Life's not so bad after all."

Later that day, after school, Sarah tells her parents about the incident. As frustrating as the whole thing was at the time, now the story makes Sarah laugh.

"Sarah," her dad says, "I never saw anyone who could roll with the punches the way you can."

"What's that mean?" she asks.

"Roll with the punches? Well," her father replies, "it started out as a boxing term. Boxers angle themselves in certain ways so that blows won't hit them as hard. So, say an opponent throws a left punch—the boxer will 'roll' with it by moving his body back and to the right. That way, even if the punch lands, it won't hurt as much as a full-contact hit. That's the way you seem to be able to handle life. Nothing really bothers you all that much. You're able to adapt yourself to whatever's happening."

"I call it being flexible," Sarah's mom puts in. "You bend with life, Sarah, instead of letting life knock you over. It's a great quality to have. And it makes life a lot easier for you. Poor Shannon has a tough time."

Sarah thinks about her friend and sighs. "I wish she could bend a little more," she tells her parents. "Everything's such a big

Life's little frustrations can knock you down if you don't have the flexibility to deal with them.

Someone who is physically flexible can stretch and bend her body easily. If you're emotionally flexible, you can emotionally stretch and bend to cope with whatever life throws at you.

deal with her. It's like every little thing that happens hits her head on and knocks her off her feet. Sometimes even *good* things make her freak out."

Sarah's dad laughs. "Nope, Shannon's definitely not a roll-with-the-punches kind of girl."

EMOTIONAL FLEXIBILITY

If your body is flexible, you can easily move, stretch, and bend. When psychologists talk about someone who has emotional flexibility, they're referring to someone like Sarah—someone who is able to "bend with life." People who are emotionally flexible are able to change and **adapt**. When life takes them by surprise, they cope without becoming upset.

According to some experts, people who are emotionally flexible are able to take a long-term rather than a short-term view

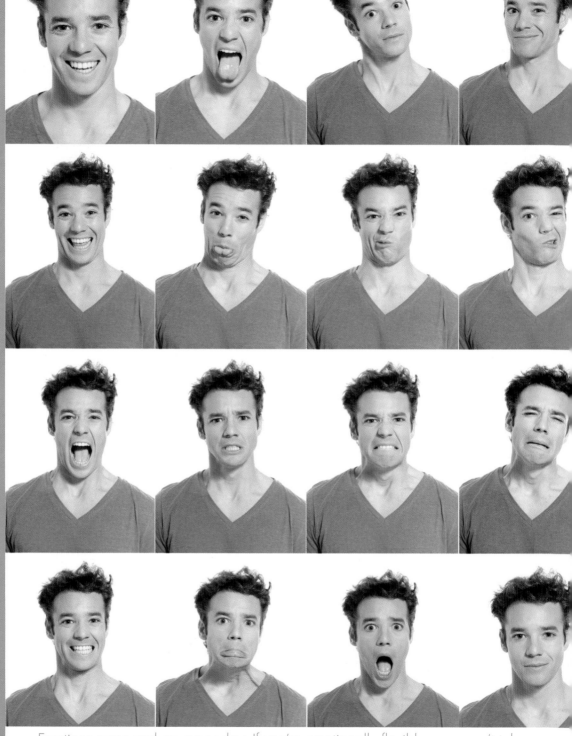

Emotions come and go every day. If you're emotionally flexible, you won't take each of them all that seriously. You'll know that pretty soon whatever you're feeling right now will change.

on life. So when something unpleasant happens—like Shannon's locker getting jammed—they understand that even though life may be *inconvenient* at the moment, by tomorrow—and certainly by next year—they'll have forgotten all about it. In the grand scheme of things, a jammed locker just isn't that big of a deal!

People with emotional flexibility also don't take their emotions too seriously. They understand that emotions come and go. Emotions are usually responses to whatever is going on right now, but they're not very *reliable* when it comes to telling anything about the long-range meaning of life.

Often, though, we feel as though our emotions tell us something about life in general. If we're happy, we feel as though life is good, while if we're sad or angry, we feel as though life is gloomy or ugly. From a scientific perspective, though, emotions are only chemical changes inside our brains. They direct us to pay attention to whatever's going on, to take action, to get help—but they don't really tell us whether life is good or bad. Emotions have more to do with what's going on *inside* us, rather than what's going on in the outside world.

ACCEPTING YOUR EMOTIONS

All this doesn't mean that emotionally flexible people try to deny their emotions. If they're unhappy, they don't pretend they're happy, and if they feel angry, they don't paste on a smile and stuff their anger out of sight. Instead, they take note of their emotions. They look for the real reason behind their feelings. For example, when Shannon fell apart emotionally after she couldn't open her locker, maybe the real reason for her extreme reaction had to do with the fact that she didn't get enough sleep the night before. She probably was also still on edge because of the fight she had with her mother before school. Or maybe she's at a point in her menstrual cycle where she tends to be more moody than usual.

But Shannon doesn't think about any of those things. For her, the jammed locker is a very, very big deal. She believes it's a

Our interactions with others are some of the things that shape our emotions—and all relationships have their ups and downs. You can be having a good time with your friends one moment. . .

. . . and have your feelings hurt the next. If you're emotionally flexible, you'll realize that lots of factors go into your emotional reaction. You may be more sensitive, for example, because you're feeling a little sick—or maybe you're upset about something else. Give it some time and you'll feel better.

sign that life is terrible. Meanwhile, Sarah realizes that she's feeling more impatient with her friend than usual simply because she skipped breakfast. All sorts of things can go into our emotional reactions. And the more we understand them, the more flexible we'll be.

LEARNING FROM THE PRESENT MOMENT

Shannon has learned to yell and cry when life doesn't go her way. Maybe when she was little, every time she cried, her mother

How your parents responded to your emotions when you were younger is one factor that may shape how emotionally flexible you are today.

When babies are frustrated with each other, they can't talk it out. Crying is their only option—but you have other choices!

rushed to help her and comfort her. So little Shannon learned that crying and yelling was the way to respond when life didn't go the way she liked.

When you're a very young baby, crying is the only way you can let the people around you know you're unhappy, but the older you get, the more **options** you have for dealing with life. As Shannon grew older, though, instead of learning new ways to cope with life, she continued to simply dissolve into tears every time she was frustrated or unhappy. Crying doesn't really help the situation at all, of course, but it's become a habit for Shannon. Instead of learning new ways to respond, she's sticking with what worked for her when she was a very young child.

Research Project

The author mentions that Shannon may have been more likely to get upset because of where she's at in her menstrual cycle. Use the Internet or the library to find out how a woman's menstrual cycle can be connected to her emotions. Explain the chemical changes that take place before and during menstruation, and describe how these can affect a woman's moods.

Shannon has temper tantrums when life doesn't go her way. Another person might eat junk food to ease her stress, or she might stare mindlessly at the television for hours at a time. Someone else might smoke or drink alcohol. People who are emotionally flexible, though, are faster to learn new and healthier responses to situations. They see each moment as something new to which they can respond creatively, coming up with new solutions.

According to psychologist Dr. Kathy Baur:

> Psychological flexibility is our ability to respond to the events in our lives, based on what's happening at that very moment, not through the filter of our past. . . . Psychological flexibility helps people develop and maintain healthy habits by loosening up their habitual responses, like stress eating, smoking, watching TV, so they can develop a more effective *repertoire* of behaviors.

COPING

The next day at school, Sarah is in a good mood. She made sure to leave time for breakfast, and she has a new understanding of why Shannon reacts the way she does to little things.

Text-Dependent Questions

1. Explain what the phrase "roll with the punches" means. How does it connect to emotional flexibility?

2. List three characteristics of people who are emotionally flexible.

3. According to this chapter, what role can habit play in how we respond to surprise?

4. Describe the differences between Sarah and Shannon in terms of emotional flexibility.

So when Shannon has a mini-tantrum when she spills milk on her shirt during lunch, Sarah just laughs. She grabs a napkin and wipes off the milk before it even soaks into the fabric.

"There, Shannon. All better."

"Thanks, Sarah." Her friend gives her a wobbly grin. "I wish I could be more like you. Your life just seems so easy compared to mine."

Of course, Sarah's life isn't really any easier than Shannon's. Being emotionally flexible doesn't make your life actually better. It just helps you cope with life more easily. Unpleasant surprises—like jammed lockers and spilled milk—don't make you think life is terrible. You just try the locker combination one more time. You wipe up the milk. You cope with the surprise, whatever it is. And then you get on with life.

Words to Understand

challenge: Something that is difficult and tests your abilities.

dilate: When something circular like a blood vessel or the pupil of your eye gets bigger.

chronic: Lasting for a long time.

nutrition: The parts of food that our bodies use to function correctly.

ulcers: Sores inside your stomach.

immune systems: The parts of our bodies that fight off disease.

anxiety: A feeling of fear or worry.

depression: A strong feeling of sadness or hopeless, which often lasts for a long time.

inevitable: Definitely going to happen, sooner or later.

THREE

HOW ARE SURPRISE AND FLEXIBILITY CONNECTED?

Surprise is the emotion we feel when life doesn't go the way we expected it to. It usually only lasts a few minutes. Flexibility has to do with what we do next, after the surprise. The flexible person is able to cope with life's surprises without becoming too stressed.

WHAT IS STRESS?

When people talk about "stress," they mean the way they feel when they can't easily handle all the unexpected things life has sent their way. Anything unexpected that poses a challenge to a person's well-being—like an illness, a death, or a divorce in the family—causes stress. Big surprises like these cause big stress, but even little surprises can pile up and cause stress as well. When lots of unexpected things happen at once—say you start a new

When you're stressed, even small frustrations can seem overwhelming.

Make Connections

Sometimes, even good surprises can cause stress. Imagine you come home from school and discover that your family has a new puppy. The same night, your favorite uncle unexpectedly drops in for dinner. While you're eating dinner, the boy or girl you've had a crush on for the past year calls you out of the blue and wants to go to a movie with you. You've just hung up on the phone (with a goofy grin on your face), when the phone rings again; this time, it's your best friend saying that he's gotten two tickets for the concert you thought was sold out. All those things are wonderful surprises. In fact, your life couldn't be better!

So when you go to bed that night, why can't you fall asleep? Why is your heart pounding and your stomach hurting? It's because your body doesn't know the difference between "bad" and "good" surprises. It just knows that you're being faced with one surprise after another. Even though all the surprises are good ones, your body is responding with the same fight-or-flight response it uses to handle danger.

job, your girlfriend suddenly breaks up with you, and your teacher decides to have a pop quiz, all on the same day—that's when surprise can turn into stress.

Stress is a normal and natural part of life. That's because none of us can control what happens in life. We can do our best to make good plans, but sooner or later, something will happen that will upset all our plans.

FIGHT-OR-FLIGHT

Surprise causes our bodies' startle response, which normally only lasts a few seconds. After that, everything should go back

The dangers you face today aren't the same as this guy's—but your body responds the same way human bodies have been responding since prehistoric days.

to normal. If that doesn't happen, however, our bodies may go into what psychologists refer to as the "fight-or-flight response." This response is the body's natural reaction to an ongoing *challenge*.

When this response was evolving, thousands and thousands of years ago, surprises were often dangerous. For example, imagine your long-ago, prehistoric ancestor minding his own business, gathering nuts and berries in the woods. Suddenly, a saber-toothed tiger leaps in front of him. Your ancestor is surprised, but his startle response almost immediately shifts into something else. If he's not going to be killed by the tiger, he had better do something fast! He can either attack the tiger with a big stick, or he can run away—fight or flight.

While he's making up his mind, his brain has already automatically sent out messages to the rest of his body, getting him ready. His body's reaction is a lot like what happens during the startle response, but it lasts longer. His heart beats harder, and he breathes faster, sending more oxygen to his muscles. His digestion slows down, while his blood pressure increases, so that more blood goes to the muscles in his arms and legs. His pupils *dilate* so he can see better. His muscles tense, getting him ready for action. And then he either starts swinging the stick—or he runs as fast as he can!

In today's world, danger is often not quite as simple as what our prehistoric ancestors faced—but our bodies don't know that. They still get ready for fight or flight, the same way human bodies have been doing for thousands and thousands of years. When stress doesn't last very long, the fight-or-flight reaction can help you deal with whatever's coming at you. On the day your girlfriend breaks up with you, you have to take a couple of unexpected quizzes, and you start a new job, the stress may feel uncomfortable, but your body's response will help you get through your terrible day. The fight-or-flight response will also help you deal with an emergency. That's what it's made for.

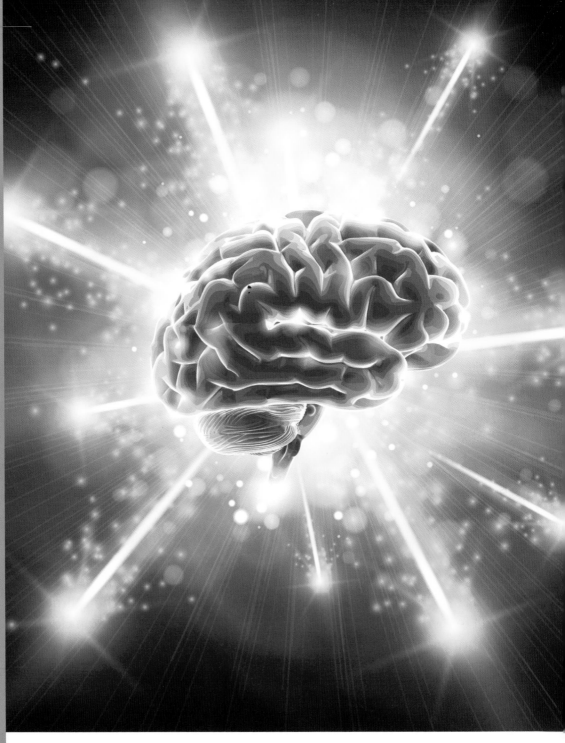

The brain's reactions are designed to help your body cope with life—but when too much life comes all at once, the brain can swamp your body with too many chemicals. Your brain needs a break—and so do you!

TOO MUCH STRESS

Your body responds to a crisis with a flood of brain chemicals that trigger changes throughout your body. Once the crisis is over, the brain and the rest of the body go back to normal. Your prehistoric ancestor either killed the saber-toothed tiger or escaped from it safely. The fight-or-flight response wasn't designed to continue for long periods of time. It was meant for short periods. That tiger didn't chase your ancestor day after day after day!

In today's world, though, we talk about *chronic* stress. It doesn't go away. Sometimes, life just keeps coming at us, presenting us with seemingly endless surprises. Chronic stress like this can create problems for us.

The brain chemicals that are so good at getting our bodies ready to fight or run away aren't so good for long-term situations. They can make our digestive systems not work the way they're supposed to, so that we either eat too much and gain weight—or eat too little and don't get the *nutrition* our bodies need to be healthy. The stress can make our stomachs produce too much acid, giving us stomachaches. If this goes on too long, we might get *ulcers* or develop some other painful condition in our digestive system. Stress reactions can also make our *immune systems* not work as well, so we're more likely to get sick more often (which, of course, is just one more unpleasant surprise!). Too much stress can also upset the balance of chemicals within our brains, causing emotional disorders like *anxiety* and *depression*. And on top of all that, we may not be able to sleep very well. The fight-or-flight response is meant to make us more alert than usual, so we can deal with danger—but that extra alertness is a bad thing when it goes on day after day. Our bodies and brains need sleep in order to heal themselves and function normally, so not sleeping just makes worse all the other problems that go along with chronic stress.

The chapter says that too much stress can cause depression and anxiety. Use the Internet or the library to find our more about depression or anxiety. What are the symptoms? What happens inside the brain? How does stress make this emotional disorder more likely to occur? Write a paragraph to answer each question.

FLEXIBILITY AND STRESS

Stress is normal—and it's *inevitable*. Sooner or later, we're all going to experience stress. Even someone like Sarah, who "rolls with the punches," will feel stressed when too many unexpected things come at her at once—or if something really big happens, like the death of someone she loves. But someone like Sarah, who is emotionally flexible, will be able to cope with stress better than someone like Shannon. And for people like Sarah, surprises don't automatically turn into stresses the way they do for Shannon. Emotionally flexible people can handle life's little surprises without getting stressed.

Psychologists tell us that people who are emotionally inflexible end up feeling sad and worried more of the time than people do who are emotionally flexible. Without emotional flexibility, feelings of sadness and worry may turn into emotional disorders like depression and anxiety, which last longer than normal emotions that come and go. When people who are emotionally inflexible have too much stress, it can get in the way of their school and work performance. They're more likely to turn to unhealthy ways of relieving stress, like overeating or abusing alcohol or drugs.

Psychologists have found that simply understanding how stress

Text-Dependent Questions

1. How does the author define stress and its causes?

2. What is the fight-or-flight response? List the changes that take place in the body during this response.

3. Define the word "chronic" and explain why chronic stress is hard on the body.

4. According to this chapter, how does emotional flexibility help people deal with stress?

affects the body can help people become more emotionally flexible. By being aware that we're stressed, we can understand what's going on and make allowances for ourselves. We can give ourselves a break and look for ways to reduce our stress levels. We may even be able to learn from life's surprises.

How Are Surprise and Flexibility Connected?

Words to Understand

pituitary gland: A gland in your head that controls how fast you grow, as well as many other body processes.

self-esteem: How good you feel about yourself.

optimism: Hopefulness and confidence about the future.

strategy: A technique or plan for handling a situation.

capacity: The ability or power to do something.

assumptions: Things you accept as true, without proof.

FOUR

WHAT CAN YOU LEARN FROM LIFE'S SURPRISES?

Have you ever heard the expression, "When all you have is a hammer, everything you see looks like a nail"? This saying describes someone who lacks emotional flexibility. Whenever he's surprised by life, he responds in the same way. If he's someone like Shannon, for example, he might scream and cry and have a tantrum. Someone else might light up a cigarette—or head for the Ben and Jerry's she knows is in the freezer. Another person might pull away from everyone and hole up in his room all by himself. Or he might do the exact opposite and start talking and laughing so loudly that everyone in the room has to pay attention to him. Whatever a person's "hammer" is, she uses it every time she runs into one of life's surprises.

But we're better off if we have an entire toolbox to choose from when we run into the unexpected things in life. If we have an assortment of coping skills, we'll be more emotionally flexible—and we'll be able to handle life a little more easily.

Here are some of the best coping skills to keep in your "toolbox." Next time you feel yourself about to reach for whatever "hammer" you've been using to cope with life's surprises, try one of these instead. And if one doesn't work this time, try another. Different people and different situations may need different coping tools.

A SENSE OF PERSPECTIVE

Remember that emotions are short-term responses that take place in your brain. Pay attention to them. Try to understand them. Ask yourself if there's something in your life that needs to change, or if there's some action you need to take. But keep in mind that whatever you are feeling right now will fade away and be replaced by some other emotion. If you're unhappy or frustrated right now, you'll feel very differently in just an hour or two. Sometimes all you need to do is wait it out! Give yourself some time, and things may look a lot better.

A SENSE OF HUMOR

You probably don't need a scientist to tell you that laughing is fun! But scientists' research has proven that laughter actually changes the chemicals inside people's brains. When people laugh, certain chemicals are released inside the brain's cells that make them feel better about life.

Your brain is made up of a network of cells called neurons that process huge quantities of information every second. Neurons pass messages from one cell to another. Picture a whole string of football players, passing a football between them, and you'll have a very rough picture of how neurons work. Neurons use chemicals called neurotransmitters to carry the message—the "football"—across the tiny gaps between each cell. The chemicals allow all the parts of the brain to communicate with each other and with the rest of the body.

There are several kinds of neurotransmitters, but one of the most important is dopamine. Dopamine is connected to good feelings. Certain behaviors cause your brain to reward you with a burst of dopamine, giving you a happy feeling of pleasure. This teaches your brain to want to do that particular behavior again and again. Laughter makes your brain release dopamine.

Endorphins are another kind of neurotransmitter. They are usually produced as a response to certain stimuli, especially stress, fear, or pain. They come from various parts of your body, the *pituitary gland*, your spinal cord, and throughout other parts of your brain and nervous system—but they end up in your brain. There, they do their job by connecting with cells in the parts of the brain responsible for blocking pain and controlling emotion. Laughter is one of the things that trigger the release of endorphins within your body. This means that if you can find something to laugh about, even physical pain won't hurt as badly—and life's unpleasant surprises won't seem as serious.

Researchers have found that when you even pretend you think something is funny—by laughing or smiling widely—you'll "trick" your body into responding the same way it would if you were genuinely amused. In fact, according to a recent study, people end up being more amused by life when they make themselves smile!

Scientific research has found that laughter has the following positive results:

- an increased ability to relax
- decreased stress levels
- increased creativity
- improved problem-solving ability
- better memory
- improved mood and feelings of well-being
- reduced depression, anxiety, and tension

Playing a quick pick-up game every day after school is one way to improve your ability to handle whatever life throws at you. Regular exercise makes your body—and brain—handle stress more easily.

Make Connections

Researchers have found that one of the effects that regular exercise has is that it reduces anxiety and depression. Experts believe that the reason exercise has this effect is that it increases the body's ability to respond to stress. It gives the body the chance to practice—and get better at—dealing with stress by forcing all the body's systems to communicate with each other more closely than usual. In other words, your cardiovascular system communicates with your muscles, which communicate with your kidneys and digestive system, all of which is controlled by your nervous system. This workout of your body's communication system is one of the greatest benefits exercise gives you. And the less you exercise, researchers have found, the more poorly your body will respond to stress. It doesn't matter what kind of exercise you choose—just get out there and move!

- increased *self-esteem*
- increased sense of hope and *optimism*
- increased energy
- feelings of greater closeness with friends and family

So next time you're surprised by life—try bursting into laughter!

ACCEPT DIFFERENCES OF OPINION

Face it—the other people in your life are often the source of some of life's most difficult surprises. You may have your life all mapped out, but your friends and family don't always cooperate with your plans. When that happens, it's easy to feel frustrated and angry. Disagreements with the people close to you make you face how little control you really have.

Fighting with your parents is never fun—but it could actually be a chance for you to prove to them that you're more emotionally mature than they think. Think of arguments as opportunities!

Make Connections

When researchers studied people with good emotional flexibility, they found that these people usually use distraction to help them cope with big surprises—things that could be very upsetting to them—while they use reappraisal to handle things that are only a little upsetting. It's all about picking the right "tool" from your toolbox!

People who are emotionally flexible, however, are able to see disagreements as opportunities rather than as something totally bad. Even though an argument with your best friend or your mother can be painful, if you can work through to the other side, you may find that your relationship is even stronger than it was before.

According to psychologist Dr. Mark Ettensohn,

Psychologists call relationship disagreements "ruptures." The great thing about ruptures is that they present us with the opportunity for repair. Repair is the process of learning to bend without breaking, to stretch our capacities for acceptance, forgiveness, and love. Through repair, we push beyond barriers and deepen our connection with another person. We are moved out of our comfort zones. . . . So the next time you find yourself in a disagreement with someone you care about, consider the opportunity that has presented itself. . . . Ask yourself what ideas you are applying about how people are supposed to act and feel, and consider the possibility that those ideas can bend without breaking. Relationships are all about growth. Any physical trainer will tell you that muscles don't grow without the muscle fibers

Make Connections

In a 2007 study, psychologist Michelle Chouinard found that when young children between one and five years old were talking with an adult, they asked an average of 76 questions an hour. According to Chouinard, "Question-asking is not something that children do every now and then—asking questions is a central part of what it means to be a child."

first being torn. It is the process of repair that makes the muscle stronger. Similarly, people don't grow without first being stretched beyond their comfort zones.

So when it comes to your relationships with others, be willing to be flexible—and you may be surprised to find that you learn and grow in ways you never expected.

THINK ABOUT SOMETHING ELSE

Sometimes when we're upset, the best thing we can do is to think about something else for a little while. Take Shannon's jammed locker. If instead of allowing herself to be swamped with frustration, Shannon had focused on the good time she and Sarah were planning for the weekend, she probably wouldn't have collapsed into tears. She would have been able to do whatever she needed to do to address the problem at hand—her jammed locker—without having an emotional meltdown.

This "tool" for coping with an unpleasant surprise—a **strategy** psychologists sometimes refer to as "distraction"—isn't meant to be permanent. With many of life's surprises, sooner or later you'll have to deal with whatever has happened. But chances are when you come back to the situation, it may not look quite so serious.

Make Connections

A 2005 study reported in the journal *Health Psychology* found that higher levels of curiosity go along with a lower chance of having high blood pressure or diabetes.

If you give yourself time by focusing on something else, your emotional response won't be as intense.

LOOK AT THINGS A LITTLE DIFFERENTLY

Psychologists call this technique for handling an unexpected situation "reappraisal." It involves thinking about the situation in a more positive light. It means you downplay the seriousness of whatever has happened. Say you're late for class, and you know your teacher is likely to be angry with you. Instead of telling yourself, "This is TERRIBLE! I am in SUCH trouble!" you might say, "This is the first time all year I've been late. Even if the teacher is angry, she'll get over it. It's really not that big of a deal."

TAKE ACTION

Think back again to Shannon's jammed locker. As soon as her locker refused to open, Shannon gave up. She collapsed in a flood of frustrated tears. Meanwhile, Sarah simply tried the combination one more time, and this time it worked.

Sometimes that's all it takes—just try something again. Other times, we may have to come up with a new approach. We may need to try something different from what we've done in the past. But in order to do that, we'll need to set aside our negative emotions. We put them on hold while we take action.

SURPRISE AND FLEXIBILITY

You may not think of "interest" as an emotion, but psychologists and neuroscientists consider it to be one of the most basic of our emotions. It's connected to the emotions of both curiosity and surprise. Interest may be the very first emotion we experience. Even newborn babies show intense interest in their mothers' faces, especially their eyes.

CREATIVITY AND CURIOSITY

When you think of the word "creativity," you may connect it to artists, poets, and musicians. Expressing yourself artistically, through images, words, or music, is certainly one way of being creative. But creativity is more than that. Psychologists say that creativity is the ability to come up with new ideas and new connections between ideas. Creative people find new ways to solve problems of all shapes and sizes. Whether or not they're artistic, all human beings have the *capacity* to be creative.

Researchers have found that creativity is linked with positive emotions. It's also linked to curiosity. When we are willing to "look outside the box" and discover something new, we're happier. We're less likely to respond to life's unexpected and unpleasant surprises with negative emotions like fear, anger, sadness, or anxiety. Positive emotions and creativity make us feel interested in the world around us. Instead of responding negatively to the unexpected, we can allow it to awaken our curiosity.

Human beings are born curious. Curiosity is how a baby learns about the world. "What's this thing? What does it feel like? What will it taste like if I put it in my mouth? What is the word that goes with it?" A baby's mind is full of questions!

Make Connections

Psychologists sometimes talk about "resilience," which is closely connected to emotional flexibility. Someone who is resilient is able to cope with stress. She adapts to even life's most unpleasant surprises—such as death, disasters, and catastrophes. Being resilient doesn't mean you go through life without feeling any stress or pain—but if you're resilient, you're able to work through your pain. You find a way to cope with life's challenges.

Resilience isn't something you're born with—and it doesn't mean you're a good person or a bad person. You usually learn resilience, though, as you grow older. Your friends and family may help you. Your culture, your religion, and your community may also give you the strength you need to become more resilient.

Young children have no rules yet for how life should be. They're open and curious about everything. Every moment of every day is interesting. As we get older, though, sometimes we stop being curious. Instead of having an open mind about the world, we often think we already know the way things are—or at least, the way they *ought* to be. We learn to judge and make **assumptions**. We get busy and we hurry through life. The ability to be fascinated, to want to explore and discover new things, however, makes us more open to life's surprises. Curiosity also helps us learn new skills, perspectives, and ideas, all of which may give us still more tools we can use for coping with life's surprises.

A creative person asks questions. She challenges her assumptions. Often she learns even more from looking for an answer than she does by finding it. Questions allow her to get involved with the world around her. She is interested in everything.

SURPRISE AND FLEXIBILITY

Research Project

This chapter compares neurons and neurotransmitters to football players. Use the Internet or the library to find out more about neurotransmitters. Draw a picture of their action (using either nerve cells or football players in your picture), labeling each step.

ACCEPTANCE

One of the most powerful tools for dealing with life's difficult surprises is to simply accept whatever happens. This means that instead of saying to yourself, "This is WRONG! This is not the way things are supposed to be!" you simply let go of those ideas and take life as it comes.

This doesn't mean you give up and do nothing. If your locker won't open, you don't say, "Oh well, my locker won't open," and walk away. Instead, you take whatever action you can. But even while you do that, you accept the situation. You don't deny it. You don't say, "It's not fair!" You open yourself to it—and see what happens next.

PAUSE

One of the best things you can do when you're confronted with a surprise is to simply pause before you react. This gives you time to think about what you do next. You don't have to reach for the "hammer" you've always used in the past. You can choose to try out another strategy instead. Experiment. See what happens.

Text-Dependent Questions

1. According to this chapter, how can humor help you cope with surprise?

2. Explain why neurons need neurotransmitters in order to do their job?

3. What are dopamine and endorphins—and what job do they do in your body? How are they related to humor?

4. List five benefits of laughter.

5. What is the difference between "distraction" and "reappraisal" as coping strategies?

6. Explain the roles that creativity and curiosity play in emotional flexibility.

Each time you're confronted with a surprise, tell yourself, "This is an opportunity, a chance to be curious, to be creative, to think about things differently, to accept something new." Be flexible!

Find Out More

IN BOOKS

Brooks, Robert. *The Power of Resilience: Achieving Balance, Confidence, and Personal Strength in Your Life.* New York: McGraw-Hill, 2004.

Merrell, Kenneth. *Strong Teens.* Baltimore, Md.: Brookes, 2007.

Reivich, Karen. *The Resilience Factor: 7 Keys to Finding Your Inner Strength and Overcoming Life's Hurdles.* New York: Harmony, 2003.

Siebert, Al. *The Resiliency Advantage: Master Change, Thrive Under Pressure, and Bounce Back from Setbacks.* San Francisco, Calif.: Berrett-Koehler, 2005.

Van Dijk, Sheri. *Don't Let Your Emotions Run Your Life for Teens.* Oakland, Calif.: Instant Help, 2011.

ONLINE

How Curiosity Works
science.howstuffworks.com/life/evolution/curiosity1.htm

The Power of Curiosity and Surprise
experiencelife.com/article/the-power-of-curiosity

Series Glossary of Key Terms

adrenaline: An important body chemical that helps prepare your body for danger. Too much adrenaline can also cause stress and anxiety.

amygdala: An almond-shaped area within the brain where the flight-or-flight response takes place.

autonomic nervous system: The part of your nervous system that works without your conscious control, regulating body functions such as heartbeat, breathing, and digestion.

cognitive: Having to do with thinking and conscious mental activities.

cortex: The area of your brain where rational thinking takes place.

dopamine: A brain chemical that gives pleasure as a reward for certain activities.

endorphins: Brain chemicals that create feelings of happiness.

fight-or-flight response: Your brain's reaction to danger, which sends out messages to the rest of the body, getting it ready to either run away or fight.

hippocampus: Part of the brain's limbic system that plays an important role in memory.

hypothalamus: The brain structure that gets messages out to your body's autonomic nervous system, preparing it to face danger.

limbic system: The part of the brain where emotions are processed.

neurons: Nerve cells found in the brain, spinal cord, and throughout the body.

neurotransmitters: Chemicals that carry messages across the tiny gaps between nerve cells.

serotonin: A neurotransmitter that plays a role in happiness and depression.

stress: This feeling that life is just too much to handle can be triggered by anything that poses a threat to our well-being, including emotions, external events, and physical illnesses.

Index

About the Author & Consultant

Rosa Waters lives in New York State. She has worked as a writer for several years, producing works on health, history, and other topics.

Cindy Croft is director of the Center for Inclusive Child Care at Concordia University, St. Paul, Minnesota where she also serves as faculty in the College of Education. She is field faculty at the University of Minnesota Center for Early Education and Development program and teaches for the Minnesota on-line Eager To Learn program. She has her M.A. in education with early childhood emphasis. She has authored *The Six Keys: Strategies for Promoting Children's Mental Health in Early Childhood Programs* and co-authored *Children and Challenging Behavior: Making Inclusion Work* with Deborah Hewitt. She has worked in the early childhood field for the past twenty years.

Picture Credits